W9-BWF-447

508.315
MAR
c.l Mariner, Tom
Deserts

DATE DUE			

C.l

DESERTS

Library Edition Published 1990

Published by Marshall Cavendish Corporation
147 West Merrick Road
Freeport, Long Island
N.Y. 11520

Printed in Italy by Imago Publishing Ltd

© Marshall Cavendish Limited 1990
© Cherrytree Press Ltd 1989

Designed and produced by AS Publishing

Library of Congress Cataloging-in-Publication Data

Mariner, Tom : illustrated by bMike Atkinson.
   Deserts / by Tom Mariner,
      p. cm. – (Earth in action)
      "A Cherrytree book."
   Includes index
   Summary: Explores the physical character of the world's deserts, discussing how they are formed, their inhabitants, and their actual and potential wealth.
      ISBN 1-85435-192-3
      1. Deserts – Juvenile literature. [1. Deserts.]
   I. Atkinson, Mike, ill. II. Title. III. Series: Earth in action
   (New York, N.Y.)
   GB612,M37, 1989   89-17278
   508,315'4–dc20   CIP
                                                                                   AC

· EARTH · IN · ACTION ·

DESERTS

Tom Mariner
Illustrated by Mike Atkinson

MARSHALL CAVENDISH
NEW YORK · LONDON · TORONTO · SYDNEY

What is a Desert?

About a third of the world's land surface is desert or almost desert. A desert may be hot or cold. It may be a vast expanse of shifting sand dunes or an immense stretch of bare rock and stones. The true hot desert has an almost unbearable climate. For days on end, the thermometer can stand at 98°F (35°C). But at night the temperature plummets to around freezing point as the heat escapes to the cloudless sky.

Scientists define deserts as areas with less than 10 inches (25 cm) of rain a year. In some places, the average annual rainfall is less than half an inch. Months, even years, may go by without any rain at all. Then a violent thunderstorm may occur, and a sudden torrent floods the hard, scorched ground. Any water

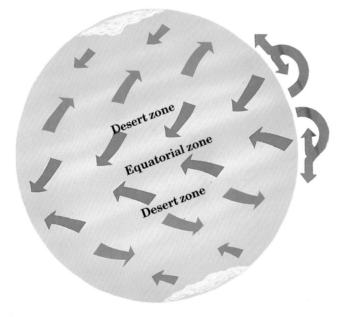

Desert zone

Equatorial zone

Desert zone

Most people's idea of a desert is of a huge sea of sand devoid of life. But deserts are not all sand – they are often rocky – and a surprising variety of living things manages to survive in them.

The air around the earth is always on the move. Its circulation is caused by the sun's heat, which is greatest at the equator. Hot air at the equator rises, spreads north and south, cools and sinks again. As it moves over the land – back toward the equator – it gets warmer and picks up moisture, so the land is kept dry. The greatest desert areas in the world lie in two zones north and south of the equator.

that does not sink into the ground is quickly dried up by winds and the sun's heat.

Deserts are barren places. Only plants and animals adapted to survive with little water can live in the harsh, dry desert world.

The world's largest deserts stretch around the world in two separate bands, between latitudes 15° and 40° North and South. In the northern hemisphere, they include the Sahara in Africa, and the Arabian, Thar and Iranian deserts in Asia. In the southern hemisphere, there are the Namib and Kalahari in Africa, the Great Desert of Australia, and the Atacama Desert in South America.

COLD DESERTS
Not all deserts are hot. Some, such as the Gobi, are hot in summer, but cold in winter. The term cold desert is also given to the lands around the North and South Poles. There is plenty of water in these areas, but most of it is frozen. The little moisture that does fall – about as much as falls in the Sahara – is in the form of snow.

Why Deserts Occur

The hottest part of the earth is at the equator. The sun heats the ground, and the hot air above it rises. It spreads north and south, cools and descends. The descending air gets warmer and picks up moisture. This creates huge regions of high pressure. The high pressure keeps out rain-bearing winds for long periods. The land and the air stay dry, and there are no clouds for most of the time.

Air gets colder as it moves up a slope. Clouds form, and rain drenches the mountainsides. When the air has crossed the crest of a mountain range, it moves down the other side. Sinking air gets warmer. It picks up moisture and dries the land, in some cases creating desert conditions. Such dry areas are said to be in a *rain shadow*.

Some deserts form near cold seas. A cold sea cools the air that passes over it. Moisture in the air collects in tiny droplets which form fog over the sea and along the coasts. But as the air moves inland, it is warmed by the hot land and becomes a drying wind.

Deserts also occur far from the sea, in the hearts of continents, where rain-bearing winds from the oceans cannot reach them. The Gobi Desert lies in central Asia, 625 miles (1000 km) from any ocean. Every wind that blows over the Gobi has crossed vast stretches of land and so has lost its moisture.

Some deserts occur because they lie in the shadow of high mountain ranges which take most of the moisture from winds which blow over them. Death Valley in California is separated from the Pacific Ocean by three mountain ranges. Winds lose moisture as they cross each range, and as a result the average rainfall each year is a mere 2½ inches (6 cm).

Some of the driest deserts are by the sea. Parts of the Atacama Desert on the western coast of South America are the driest places on earth. Winds that blow over the Atacama have crossed cold ocean currents in the Pacific. These cool winds produce fog on land, but virtually no rain.

Deserts often form in the middle of continents. Winds pick up moisture as they blow over the oceans, but lose it as they travel over the land. The heart of the vast Gobi Desert in China is 625 miles (1000 km) from the sea. It is inhabited by Mongol tribes, who travel about by means of their two-humped bactrian camels.

The Desert Landscape

It may sound strange, but much desert scenery has been formed by water. During the millions of years of its history, the earth's climate has changed many times. Many deserts once had rivers flowing across them, or had plentiful rainfall. Today's desert landscapes were shaped by the water.

Many millions of years ago, Monument Valley in Utah was a high plateau. Streams flowed across the high, flat land and carved valleys in it, which in time became deep canyons. Gradually, these valleys broadened, as more and more of the high land was worn away. Parts of the former plateau remained as tall steep-sided islands of rock called *mesas* (the Spanish word for tables), or as smaller, narrower

Monument Valley in Utah has spectacular desert scenery – worn down over millions of years by the power of a river and its tributaries. Little remains of the original river plain, except the mesas, buttes and pillars of hard rock that have defied the battering of wind, weather and water.

columns called *buttes* (the French word for mounds) and *pillars*. You can see from their height how high the original plain must have been.

The Ice Ages

For hundreds of thousands of years, northern Europe and much of North America were as cold as the polar regions. While they were in the grip of the Ice Age, the Sahara and the deserts of North America had mild, moist climates; the land was green with grass and trees. Prehistoric peoples lived there, and wild animals roamed the grassy plains. Then about 10,000 years ago, the climate became hotter, and the northern ice melted. Lands farther south became hotter and drier. The forests and the grass died, and the land turned dry and barren.

Places that were once fertile are now desert. Prehistoric hippopotamuses (below) bathed in warm pools where now there is only sand. The ancient people of the Sahara left cave paintings (above) showing cattle and wild animals that could never survive in the region now.

Water in the Desert

Rain is rare in the desert, but when it falls, it does not fall gently. Usually, freak storms occur which may bring a year's rainfall in a few hours. The quantity of rain varies from place to place. One part of the desert may be flooded, while a few miles away, there is a light shower, or no rain at all.

Rain in the desert is rare, but violent. The force of the occasional storms causes flooding. The swirling water wears out gullies, or wadis, and carries with it stones and sand, which are left in a new home when the water disappears almost as rapidly as it came.

Soil soaks up rain and holds it like a sponge until it sinks down into water-bearing rocks below the surface. Deserts have little soil. Large areas are covered by stones or bare rock. When storms break, the rainwater washes across the surface. It cascades down valley slopes, picking up rock fragments and loose stones as it goes. This mixture surges along the valley floor like a torrent of thin concrete mix. When the rain stops, the load of rocks and stones, called *alluvium*, is strewn over the desert surface.

Wadis and Fans

The brief, violent *flash floods* carve out valleys or gullies, which are called *wadis* in the Sahara and *arroyos* in North and South America. They have steep sides, and their floors are littered with stones left behind when previous floods dried up. Piles of rock fragments are dumped at the mouths of the valleys where the valleys meet broad plains. These heaps of material are called *alluvial fans*.

Out on the plain, water from the hills collects in a shallow basin, called a *playa lake*. Hot sun quickly dries up the water, leaving behind a layer of salts which had been dissolved in the water.

For months or years on end, the red soil of the Great Australian Desert bakes in the sun. Then suddenly it rains. Millions of plant seeds that have lain in wait in the soil seize their opportunity. In a frantic rush, they sprout, flower and make new seeds. Then they wither and die, and the desert is bare again.

DANGER, WADI
Signs in the Sahara warn drivers not to cross a wadi if the river is flowing. Sudden floods have been known to drown the unwary, but travelers do not have to wait long. A raging torrent can be dry land again in a few hours.

Shaping the Desert

Desert landscapes are constantly worn away, or eroded, by *weathering*. Most deserts are very hot by day and cold at night. When rocks are heated, they expand; and when they cool, they contract. Repeated expanding and contracting, even by tiny amounts, weakens solid rock and causes pieces to flake off.

Another form of weathering is caused by the small amounts of water found in deserts. Surface cracks in rocks open up when the rock gets hot, and this allows water from dew or occasional storms to get into them. The water often has salt dissolved in it. When the water is dried up by the sun, this salt is left behind. Over many years, this happens many times and slowly a layer of salt crystals forms. As the crystals grow, they force the rock apart. A piece of the surface, like a layer of onion, peels away and falls off.

The surface in some parts of the desert (right) is a thick "pavement" of stones. They have been left behind as the wind has gradually stripped away the loose sand that once separated them. Once enough sand has gone, the stones form a barrier which the strongest wind cannot lift, so the sand below is protected.

Extremes of temperature cause the surface of the desert to break up. It is very hot by day. The ground becomes baking hot. Then the temperature drops dramatically, and the ground shrinks, causing it to crack – sometimes so violently that you can hear it.

The surface of a rock gets very hot during the day, and cold at night. The shrinking of the surface causes a whole layer to peel off, like skin that has been sunburned.

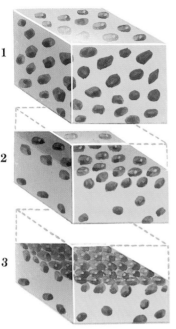

The Wind at Work

Desert winds tend to blow in the same direction for weeks on end. In places, they sweep all the loose sand away, leaving a surface of bare rock. Much of the Sahara has this surface. The Arabs call it *hamada*. Elsewhere, layers of loose stones cover the desert and form a rough surface they call *reg*.

The winds also blow sand against the rocks. Little by little, the wind-blown sand grains polish and wear away the rocks like a natural sand-blaster. But wind erosion occurs only near ground level. This is because sand grains are heavy and the winds cannot lift them much higher than a few feet. As a result, the rocks higher up are untouched. With their bases eroded and their tops not, the rocks look top-heavy and are called *mushroom rocks*. In the deserts of central Asia, there are long, low ridges of rock called *yardangs*, arranged in rows. Once there was rock between the rows, but it was softer rock, and the wind wore it away.

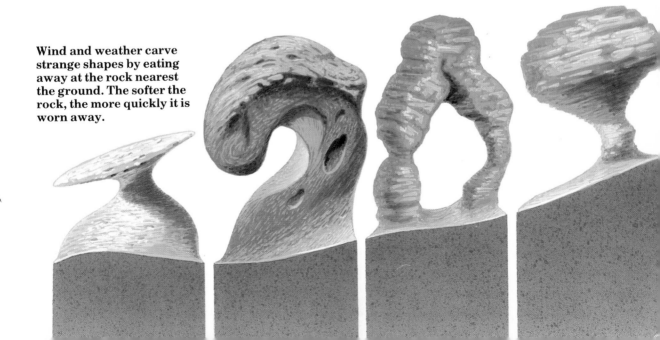

Wind and weather carve strange shapes by eating away at the rock nearest the ground. The softer the rock, the more quickly it is worn away.

Sea of Sand

In parts of some deserts, there are no rocks to be seen. The entire surface is a sea of sand. Sand deserts cover a quarter of the world's desert areas. They are called *erg* in the Sahara, where the largest areas of sand desert occur.

The sand is not flat, and it is not still. Desert winds, blowing steadily, sweep it into piles called *dunes*. If the wind meets an obstacle, such as a boulder or a small bush, it slows down and drops some of its load of

sand. In time, this sand builds up higher and higher to form a dune.

There are several kinds of dune, and they are all formed by the wind and moved by the wind. Wind picks up sand on the gentle slope of the dune and pushes it to the top. From there, the sand grains slide to the bottom of the steep slope on the other side. The wind is continuously taking sand from one side of the dune and adding to the other. In this way, the dune moves forward.

Sometimes dunes form chains many miles long which creep forward over the desert. Some dunes are 650 feet (200 m) high and may be thousands of years old.

New dunes start where something acts as a barrier to the wind. It may be something as small as a twig, but once the sand starts to pile up, the dune grows ever more rapidly. As it grows, it creeps forward.

Where does all the sand come from? It comes from soil which covers the rocks in most places. Soil is made up mostly of gravel, sand and dust. When it is damp, these particles stick together. If the climate turns dry, they separate. Dust is light and is easily swept high into the air and carried great distances by the wind. Sand is heavier, so the wind can only blow it along close to the ground. The gravel is so heavy that it hardly moves. The sand is swept away from it, leaving a surface of stones or bare rock in some places and sand dunes in others.

The shape of a sand dune depends on the prevailing winds. If winds blow from many directions, the sand piles up any which way.

Barchans are formed by the wind blowing in one direction. There is less sand at the ends than in the middle, so the sand moves faster there and an arc or crescent forms.

Seif dunes are long, narrow ridges of sand, caused when winds sometimes blow at right angles to the main wind. They may stretch for many miles.

Sometimes the wind pushes sand over the top of a crescent dune and blows it on to form a bulge in the next, so that the dunes form a staggered pattern like the seats in a theater. This pattern is called *aklé*.

Rain falling on high land sinks into the permeable rock below. The water flows through the rock under the desert. In places, the overlying rock may be worn away, allowing the water to flow out as a stream or spring and form an oasis (top). In other places, a break, or fault, may occur so that a pool forms on the surface (bottom).

Oases

An oasis is a place in the desert where there is always enough water to keep plants and animals alive. It may be a small pool or a large area with enough water to grow crops and support thousands of people.

Under many deserts, there are layers of *permeable* rocks, such as sandstone and limestone. Sandstone contains many small pores (holes) through which water can seep. Limestone contains cracks and shafts through which water can flow. Rainwater which falls on permeable rocks outside the desert seeps under the desert through the rocks. If the rocks are near the surface, wells can be dug down to them.

In places, wind-blown sand may scour out a hollow and uncover a water-bearing rock. The water then flows to the surface, and an oasis is formed.

One oasis in northeastern Algeria lies in a vast bowl scooped out of the sand by the wind. The water-bearing rock which runs under the desert comes from the Atlas Mountains more than 100 miles (160 km) away. About 20,000 people live in the oasis, most of them in the town of El Oued.

Oases that lie in hollows have to be protected from the wind, which would quickly pile sand up against the houses and plants, and eventually bury them. To hold back the sand, people often build long fences made of palm leaves tied in bunches. They set the fences in rows at right angles to the wind direction.

The soil in the fields must also be kept damp, to prevent most of it from turning to dust and being blown away.

Dates are extremely nutritious, and they grow well in a hot, dry climate. They are the most widely grown food plant in desert oases in the Middle East and North Africa. Date palm trees are about 80 feet (25 m) high and bear about 110 pounds (50 kg) of dates each year.

Plants in the Desert

Conditions in the desert are unkind to plants. During the day, they are exposed to baking temperatures and hot, dry winds. At night, they are likely to be frozen. Their main problem is shortage of water. Even when there is water, it tends to arrive in sporadic bursts.

Desert plants have developed various ways of coping with months of drought, broken by a few hours' flood. Some are drought evaders. Their seeds lie in the desert waiting for rain, sometimes for years on end. When it comes, they spring into life and grow rapidly. Within about eight weeks, they have flowered and scattered their seeds. Some seeds are protected by a hard crust that only dissolves after a thorough soaking. This prevents them from starting to grow until enough rain has fallen to keep them alive.

Other plants are drought resisters. They obtain water whenever it is available. Some have long roots that spread out just below the surface, so that they can take advantage of water flooding a wide area. Some

The Saguaro cactus resists drought by storing water in its huge body and arms.

The creosote bush stretches out its roots just below the surface to catch as much floodwater as it can before it evaporates.

Cactus plants (left) have shallow roots. They spread out to catch all the moisture they can during brief desert storms. Mesquite bushes (far left) have extremely long roots which probe deep into the sand in search of water. There is much more of a mesquite under the ground than over it.

have roots that sink deep below the ground in search of water in underlying rocks.

Many drought resisters have ways of storing water to tide them over prolonged periods of drought. Cactuses store water in their fleshy stems. They usually grow spines instead of leaves. Spines give off less water than leaves, and they deter animals that might otherwise bite into the plant and steal its water.

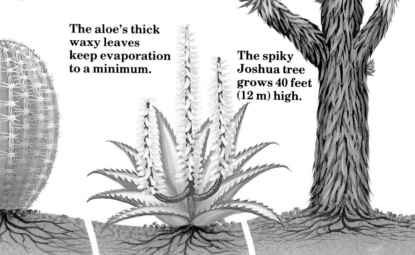

The barrel cactus swells to twice its size when it rains and gradually shrinks during droughts.

The aloe's thick waxy leaves keep evaporation to a minimum.

The spiky Joshua tree grows 40 feet (12 m) high.

At night, the North American desert (opposite) comes alive. Small creatures like the kangaroo rat come out of their burrows to find seeds or insects to eat. They listen hard for the sound of enemies like the kit fox, or the poisonous rattlesnake and Gila monster.

The Gila monster is a large poisonous lizard, with a fat tail. If it cannot find food, it can live for long periods on the fat in its tail.

Birds suffer in great heat. The cactus wren nests in the Saguaro cactus and gets moisture from its flesh. The mourning dove can go for long periods without water and flies deep into the desert.

The scorpion and the wolf spider (below) run down their prey and poison them. The spider hides in its lair until it sees a victim and makes a dash to catch it.

Wolf spider

Animals of the Desert

During the day, the desert looks like the empty place it ought to be, but at night it changes. Animals that have hidden from the sun all day come out as the temperature drops. During the day, they hide under stones or bury themselves in the sand. Half an arm's length down, the sand is cool and stays the same temperature, day or night.

When rain comes and the plants grow, millions of insect eggs and cocoons burst open, releasing adult beetles, wasps, moths, ants and locusts. Like the plants, their lives are short. They must breed and lay their eggs before they die from lack of moisture.

Reptiles, such as snakes and lizards, like warmth, but cannot stay in the heat for long. They may venture out to catch food before hurrying back to the shade. Spiders and scorpions have tough outer coatings on their bodies that prevent water loss, but both remain underground for most of the time.

Warm-blooded Creatures

Most of the mammals that live in deserts are small, burrowing rodents that live mostly on seeds scattered on the desert floor. Nearly every desert has its own jumping rodent, with powerful back legs on which to bound away from enemies. North America has the kangaroo rat, Asia the jerboa and the gerbil, and Australia the pouched kangaroo mouse.

The kit fox preys on the kangaroo rat. Like the jack rabbit, it has huge ears. Not only does this give it excellent hearing, but the ears act as radiators, giving off heat and thereby keeping the animal cool.

20

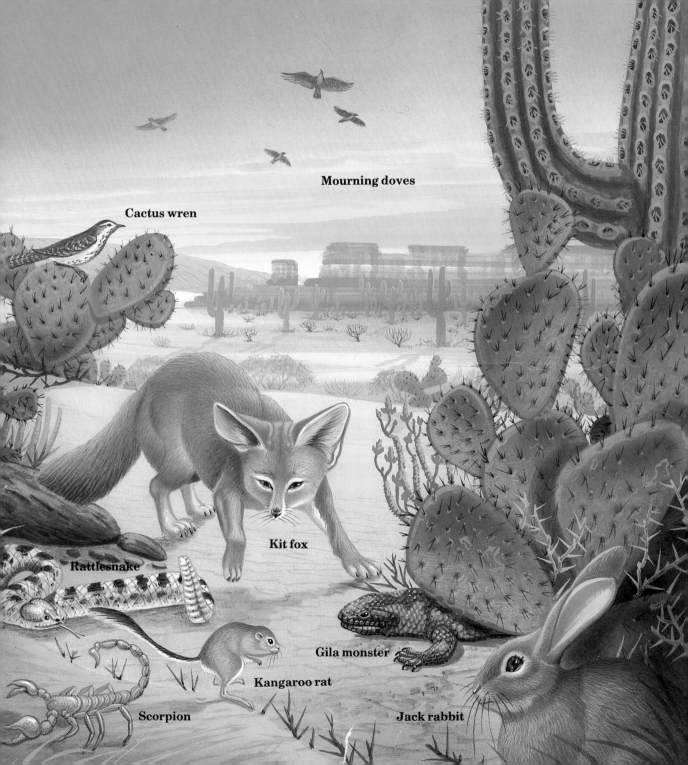

Mourning doves

Cactus wren

Kit fox

Rattlesnake

Gila monster

Scorpion

Kangaroo rat

Jack rabbit

Desert Hunters

Even though deserts are such inhospitable places, people have lived in them for thousands of years, adapting their ways to cope with the heat and the shortage of water. Today most of these desert people have given up their traditional ways of life, moving to paid jobs on farms or in towns, but a few still live just as their ancestors did. They get everything they need from the desert. They live off desert plants and hunt desert animals. They have few possessions and no settled homes. They are always on the move in search of food.

The Bushmen of the Kalahari will bring down an ostrich with a poisoned arrow. Once the animal has fallen, they spear it to death and carry it back to the family camp.

The Bushmen of the Kalahari

The Kalahari Desert is in southwestern Africa and covers parts of Botswana and Namibia. The Bushmen live in small family groups scattered over a vast area. Each group hunts and gathers its own food. In the dry season, larger groups meet and stay around any waterholes that have not dried up.

The Bushmen are skilled hunters. They use bows and arrows, clubs and spears. Their bows are too small and weak to shoot an arrow that would kill an ostrich or an antelope. Instead, they tip the arrows with poison, taken from snakes, spiders or scorpions, or made from certain poisonous plants or rocks.

While the men are away hunting, the women dig up roots and collect berries, fruits and seeds from the desert. The children catch flying ants, grubs, locusts and lizards. If they are lucky, they may bring back a puff adder to roast for the evening meal. Boys learn to hunt for birds and small creatures when they are only seven years old.

The First Australians

Like the Bushmen, the aboriginal people of Australia hunt in small groups and constantly move from place to place in search of food and water. The men hunt emu and wallabies with spears and throwing sticks. The women and children gather firewood, dig up roots and collect anything good to eat, such as grass shoots, lizards and witchetty grubs.

Following their traditional ways has become increasingly difficult for these Australians, as more and more of their land has been taken over by settlers and developed.

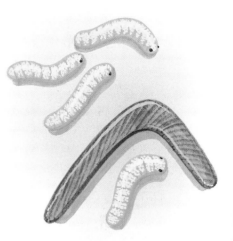

The Aborigines of Australia use a curved throwing stick, called a boomerang, to knock down birds and small animals. Some boomerangs are shaped so that, if they miss their target, they return to the thrower.
Easy to catch, though not easy to find, are the juicy witchetty grubs, a delicacy found in the roots of bushes or in crevices in trees.

Desert Farmers

Bedouin shepherds move their families, homes and flocks from pasture to pasture on the more fertile edges of the desert. Camel nomads go further into the deserts and wander far from oases.

Farming in the desert depends on the supply of water. Crops can be grown in the desert only at oases where water occurs naturally, or where water is brought to the farmland by irrigation. It takes a thousand times more water to grow palm trees than it does to keep camels, so keeping animals is more rewarding than trying to grow crops if there is no means of irrigating the land.

The Arabian camel is perfectly adapted to desert life.

It will drink salty water that would poison other animals, and it can go for a week without drinking. Fat stored in its hump breaks down to give it an indirect water supply when it needs it.

The camel has nostrils that close and long, double eyelashes that keep out dust during sandstorms.

People of the Desert

The Bedouin people are Arabs who live in the Sahara and in the desert parts of Saudi Arabia, Jordan, Syria and Iraq. Their name means "people of the desert".

The Bedouin live in small groups of about 100 people and lead a *nomadic* way of life, continually on the move. They keep sheep, goats, camels and horses. Because water and pasture in the desert are soon used up, the Bedouin and their animals rarely stay in one place for longer than a week. Unlike the Bushmen and the Australian Aborigines who travel on foot, some of the Bedouin use horses and camels for transport. The sheep and goats provide them with meat and milk, and they buy rice grown in cultivated areas. They also eat lizards, honey and locusts.

Their way of life seems difficult, but their clothes and homes are comfortable. They cover themselves from head to foot in loose-fitting robes which keep out the sand and keep them cool. The women weave goat- or camel-hair into cloth to make tents and carpets. The tents are constructed so that the few available currents of cool air can flow through them during the day. At night, the flaps are closed, and the families sleep on the carpets. When it is time to move on, they simply roll up their homes and load them on the camels.

The camel's widely spaced toes are joined by a bridge of skin that stops it from sinking into the soft sand.

Wealth of the Desert

Deserts may be inhospitable, but many of them contain rich deposits of minerals that can be mined. Desert soils also contain minerals that plants thrive on. With the addition of water, deserts can be turned into fertile agricultural land. Imperial Valley in California was once a barren waste. Now it produces record crops of fruit and vegetables – thanks to irrigation.

Water Wells and Oil Wells

Where there are water-bearing rocks under the desert, engineers dig deep wells to reach it. Part of the Sahara is irrigated in this way. In other places, water is taken from rivers and lakes. Dams are built on rivers that

Crops, such as melons, are grown under plastic tunnels. When the plants are big enough, the top of the plastic is split to allow the fruit to ripen.

cross desert regions, and the water is carried in canals to dry areas. It was the building of the Hoover Dam on the Colorado River that enabled farmers to grow crops in Imperial Valley. In Israel, water from the Sea of Galilee is transported 100 miles (160 km) by canals, tunnels and pipes to the Negev Desert.

Nowadays, the flow of water to each plant can be controlled by computers. To prevent plants from drying out in the fierce heat, many crops are grown in plastic tunnels. Instead of escaping into the air, water that evaporates from the plants condenses in the cool night temperatures and falls back on to the ground.

It is not only water that is found in rocks under the desert. More than half the world's oil comes from wells in the Arabian Desert and neighboring regions.

Oil from wells dug far into the desert is carried hundreds of miles by pipeline to refineries where it is processed. Oil brings immense wealth to a country, but in most places, little of the money reaches the needy.

27

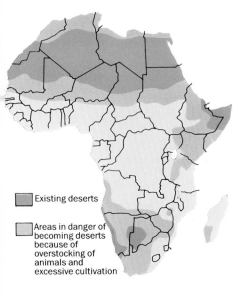

Existing deserts

Areas in danger of becoming deserts because of overstocking of animals and excessive cultivation

More and more land in Africa is turning to desert. The Sahel is semi-desert that borders the southern Sahara. Scientists estimate that winds blow 400 million tons of soil from the Sahel to the Atlantic Ocean every year.

When it rains in the desert, there is a chance for crops to grow. But locusts grow as well. Once they are airborne, nothing can stop the swarms from devouring every green leaf in sight.

Battle for the Future

Keeping deserts habitable is a constant battle. As more people move into desert areas, more and more water is needed, and providing water is expensive. Only wealthy countries can afford it, and only for as long as the water supply will last. In parts of Arizona, a ban has been imposed on the building of new swimming pools. In poorer countries, the problems are far more serious; the deserts are spreading.

Around the deserts are areas of semi-desert and *scrub*, with scanty bushes and trees. These regions have a short rainy season and usually enough rain falls for people to live by keeping animals or by growing crops. But, every year, more and more of these areas become unusable for farming, because there are too many people trying to eke a living from them. More people means more animals. The animals eat the

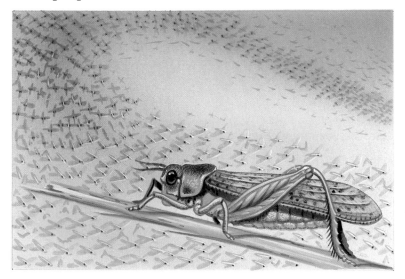

28

plants, and the people cut down trees and bushes for firewood. Without plant roots to bind the soil together, the soil crumbles to dust and the wind blows it away. Once the soil is gone, nothing will grow.

Even when people have been successful at growing crops, disaster may strike. Locusts breed in the desert and build up into vast swarms. When these swarms land, they eat every trace of growing plant life. Constant efforts are made to track the swarms and spray the newly hatched insects with insecticides before they mature and grow wings.

Elsewhere, the battle against moving sand is waged. Dunes can be held in place with oil which binds the sand grains together. Once the dune is stable, soil can be mixed with the sand. Trees are planted in the dunes to anchor them, and wells are dug to give them a supply of water. In that way, it is hoped that more and more of the desert can be brought to life.

One benefit of the oil industry is that waste oil can be sprayed over the dunes, creating a mulch in which plants can put down roots.

Desert Profiles

Major deserts appear on the map; there are many smaller deserts elsewhere, and there are individual deserts with local names within the larger areas. Names printed in *italics* indicate a separate entry. There are no deserts in Europe.

AFRICA

Kalahari Covers 200,000 sq mi (520,000 sq km) of southern Africa mainly in Botswana. The land consists of barren red sand dunes and areas of scrub or semi-desert. A variety of animals, including big game, manage to live there. The original inhabitants of the desert, the Bushmen, live by hunting.

Namib Like the *Atacama* desert of South America, this is a narrow coastal desert where fogs are common and rain is infrequent. It lies mostly in Namibia and is virtually uninhabited.

Sahara The world's largest desert, it stretches 2,000 miles (5200 km) across North Africa and covers 3,240,000 sq mi (8,400,000 sq km) – a quarter of the entire continent. Only about a tenth is sandy desert; the rest is bare rock or loose stones, and there are hilly and mountainous areas. Antelopes and other large animals live near waterholes and oases, and in some places the nomadic Bedouin still follow their traditional ways of life. Once only camel caravans could cross the Sahara.

Now, with the oil industry, travel by road is much easier.

Somali Inland desert in East Africa that covers 100,000 sq mi (260,000 sq km), occupying most of Somalia and crossing the border into Ethiopia.

AMERICAS

Atacama A narrow strip of land between the Andes and the Pacific Ocean in northern Chile is the driest desert. It is claimed that parts of the Atacama had no rain for 400 years, from 1570 to 1971. The desert covers 70,000 sq mi (180,000 sq km). Most of it is barren, but rich in minerals. A northern extension of the Atacama lies on the Pacific coast of Peru.

Great Western Once a vast area of the southwestern U.S. was barren land. Now, thanks to vast irrigation schemes, much of the land is farmed and able to support industries and large populations in the states of California, Arizona, Texas and New Mexico. Continuing south, the desert extends into Sonora and Baja California in Mexico.

Individual deserts in the region include the *Great Basin*, *Mojave*, Sonora and Chihuahua.

Great Basin Covers about 200,000 sq mi (520,000 sq km), mostly in Nevada. The desert is surrounded by high mountains. Rivers flowing from the mountains dry up, leaving salt lakes which may be dry or wet. The Great Salt Lake is the largest.

Natural vegetation is scrub with a few trees. Death Valley, in California, is a desolate trough which contains the lowest land in the western hemisphere. The area is of spectacular beauty, rich in minerals and wildlife.

Mojave Area in southeastern California which covers about 25,000 sq mi (65,000 sq km) between the Sierra Nevada mountains and the Colorado River. The vegetation is mainly desert scrub, consisting of creosote bushes and Joshua trees.

Patagonia This region near the tip of South America is both in Chile and in Argentina. It covers about 300,000 sq mi (770,000 sq km) and is a cold desert plateau, similar to the Gobi. Only the valleys of rivers which rise in the Andes are fertile.

ASIA

Arabian Eastward continuation of the *Sahara* stretching from the Red Sea, through Saudi Arabia, to Iran. In the north it includes parts of Jordan, Israel, Iraq and Syria. In all it covers 500,000 sq mi (1,300,000 sq km).

Gobi High plateau region in central Asia which covers more than 400,000 sq mi (1,000,000 sq km) of northern China and Mongolia. The desert is hot in summer, but the winters are long and bitterly cold. The few people who live in the desert are Mongolian nomads who herd cattle – long-haired yaks – and travel with camels. They live in warm tents called yurts.

Kara Kum (and Kyzyl Kum) West of the *Gobi* and *Takla Makan* deserts and east of the Caspian Sea in the U.S.S.R. lie these two deserts, which are separated by the Amu Darya

Deserts of the World

River. They cover 200,000 sq mi (520,000 sq km). Irrigation schemes allow both deserts to grow crops, and herdsmen raise sheep, goats and camels.

Takla Makan Desert in central Asia, west of the *Gobi*. It covers 175,000 sq mi (450,000 sq km) and is mainly drifting sand dunes, which make its interior almost uninhabitable. Temperatures are extreme, ranging from −13°F (−25°C) in winter to 88°F (30°C) in summer.

Thar Sandy desert that runs from northwestern India into Pakistan. Most of the desert is barren waste or scrub, but in some places there is enough rainfall to grow grass for grazing. Parts are also irrigated. There is one large town, Jodhpur, and many small villages.

AUSTRALIA

Great Australian Desert covers 600,000 sq mi (1,550,000 sq km) in central and western Australia. An additional 550,000 sq mi (1,450,000 sq km) is semi-desert making 1,200,000 sq mi (3,000,000 sq km), about 39 percent of Australia. There are dry rivers and salt lakes.

Kangaroos and other marsupials can survive in the less barren areas. Rain is infrequent, but if enough falls, the desert blooms as dormant seeds take root and flower.

Few people live in the desert except for those aboriginal people who still live by hunting and gathering, and the inhabitants of isolated mining towns.

Individual deserts are the

Great Sandy, the Gibson, and the Great Victoria.

POLAR REGIONS

Arctic Around the Arctic Ocean at the North Pole there is a ring of cold lands. These frozen wastes cover parts of Canada, Alaska, Greenland and Siberia in the U.S.S.R. Mosses and lichens and low shrubs grow in snowfree areas, and flowers bloom in the brief summer.

Antarctica This roughly circular continent is larger than Europe and is so cold and barren that it can support no life except for a few plants around its edge.

31

Index

For individual deserts, refer also to pages 30 and 31. See also map on page 31.